This SideKick belongs to:

____

If found, please call:

(   )   -
____

The TurboCharged SideKick

Dian Griesel, Ph.D. & Tom Griesel

THE BUSINESS SCHOOL OF HAPPINESS
CONNECTICUT

with every mouthful of food and note when you ate it. Record when and if you are drinking plenty of water to fill your tank. Record your mini-muscle exercises and other activities to make sure you are covering not just those arms that you want to look fabulous in a t-shirt, but your abdominals, back muscles, legs and butt muscles as well.

Note your moods. Is it time to practice Step 8 more often? Maybe re-read The TurboCharged Mind and listen to some of the download meditations to stay relaxed, focused and on track?

Keeping track of your actions will help you reach your goal of a TurboCharged body and keep you healthier and lean for life. It becomes particularly valuable when ordinary life seems temporarily suspended—like at holiday times and vacations, for example.

Keep this handy. Record your progress. Add photos. Keep it real. This is yours and yours alone. You don't have to ever share this information with anyone. Be true to yourself and you will be reaping the rewards of being TurboCharged. Share your progress and challenges with us via our facebook.com/turbochargedUS page and do log in often at our website at turbocharged.US.com. Most of all—keep living and find fun everyday. Make it a TurboCharged Day!

With best wishes for your ongoing success,
Dian & Tom

MONTHLY PROFILE

Date: *Body Fat:* %

Height: *Neck:* *Waist:* *Hip:* *Weight:*

PLACE PHOTO HERE

Notes

WEEK 1 - MONDAY

Today's Date: | *Today's Weight:* | *Today's Body Fat:* %

Food Log

Time: | *Food Choice:* | *# of:* Fruits | Veggies | Proteins

Today's Total:

Water Log

# of 8-oz. glasses:

1	2	3	4
5	6	7	8
9	10	11	12
13	14	15	16

Energy Log

	Morning	*Afternoon*	*Evening*
High			
Med.			
Low			

Mini-Muscle Sets & Activity Log

 # of: Minutes

Activity 1:

Activity 2:

Activity 3:

Activity 4:

Activity 5:

Extra Activities:

Today's Total:

TURBOTIP

At the starting line, the most important things are food separation and unlimited amounts of fruits, followed by vegetables and a protein meal daily.

Notes

Today's Date: *Today's Weight:* *Today's Body Fat:* %

WEEK 1 - TUESDAY

Food Log

Time: *Food Choice:*

\# of: Fruits Veggies Proteins

Today's Total:

Mini-Muscle Sets & Activity Log

\# of: Minutes

Activity 1:

Activity 2:

Activity 3:

Activity 4:

Activity 5:

Extra Activities:

Today's Total:

Water Log

# of 8-oz. glasses:

1	2	3	4
5	6	7	8
9	10	11	12
13	14	15	16

Energy Log

	Morning	*Afternoon*	*Evening*
High			
Med.			
Low			

Notes

WEEK 1 - WEDNESDAY

Today's Date: | *Today's Weight:* | *Today's Body Fat:* %

Food Log

Time:	*Food Choice:*	# of: Fruits	Veggies	Proteins
	Today's Total:			

Water Log

# of 8-oz. glasses:

1	2	3	4
5	6	7	8
9	10	11	12
13	14	15	16

Energy Log

	Morning	Afternoon	Evening
High			
Med.			
Low			

Mini-Muscle Sets & Activity Log

	# of: Minutes
Activity 1:	
Activity 2:	
Activity 3:	
Activity 4:	
Activity 5:	
Extra Activities:	
Today's Total:	

Notes

Today's Date: *Today's Weight:* *Today's Body Fat:* %

WEEK 1 - THURSDAY

Food Log

 # of: Fruits Veggies Proteins

Time: *Food Choice:*

Today's Total:

Mini-Muscle Sets & Activity Log

 # of: Minutes

Activity 1:

Activity 2:

Activity 3:

Activity 4:

Activity 5:

Extra Activities:

Today's Total:

Water Log

# of 8-oz. glasses:

1	2	3	4
5	6	7	8
9	10	11	12
13	14	15	16

Energy Log

	Morning	*Afternoon*	*Evening*
High			
Med.			
Low			

Notes

WEEK 1 - FRIDAY

Today's Date: *Today's Weight:* *Today's Body Fat:* %

Food Log

Time:	*Food Choice:*	# of: Fruits	Veggies	Proteins
	Today's Total:			

Water Log

# of 8-oz. glasses:

1	2	3	4
5	6	7	8
9	10	11	12
13	14	15	16

Energy Log

	Morning	Afternoon	Evening
High			
Med.			
Low			

Mini-Muscle Sets & Activity Log

	# of: Minutes
Activity 1:	
Activity 2:	
Activity 3:	
Activity 4:	
Activity 5:	
Extra Activities:	
Today's Total:	

Notes

Today's Date: | *Today's Weight:* | *Today's Body Fat:* %

WEEK 1 - SATURDAY

Food Log

Time:	*Food Choice:*	# of: Fruits	Veggies	Proteins
	Today's Total:			

Mini-Muscle Sets & Activity Log

	# of: Minutes
Activity 1:	
Activity 2:	
Activity 3:	
Activity 4:	
Activity 5:	
Extra Activities:	
Today's Total:	

Water Log

# of 8-oz. glasses:

1	2	3	4
5	6	7	8
9	10	11	12
13	14	15	16

Energy Log

	Morning	*Afternoon*	*Evening*
High			
Med.			
Low			

Notes

WEEK 1 - SUNDAY

Today's Date: *Today's Weight:* *Today's Body Fat:* %

Food Log

Time:	*Food Choice:*	# of: Fruits	Veggies	Proteins
	Today's Total:			

Water Log

# of 8-oz. glasses:

1	2	3	4
5	6	7	8
9	10	11	12
13	14	15	16

Energy Log

	Morning	*Afternoon*	*Evening*
High			
Med.			
Low			

Mini-Muscle Sets & Activity Log

	# of: Minutes
Activity 1:	
Activity 2:	
Activity 3:	
Activity 4:	
Activity 5:	
Extra Activities:	
Today's Total:	

Notes

WEEK 1 PROGRESS

Activity Wrap-up

Did you meet your activity and mini-muscle strengthening goals for the week?

Starting Weight:

Ending Weight:

Starting Body Fat: %

Ending Body Fat: %

Food Wrap-up

Did you meet your food intake goals for the week?

Energy Wrap-up

Overall, how was your energy level this week?

High ☐

Med. ☐

Low ☐

Goals for Next Week

What things would you like to improve on for next week?

WEEK 2 - MONDAY

Today's Date: | *Today's Weight:* | *Today's Body Fat:* %

Food Log

Time:	*Food Choice:*	Fruits	Veggies	Proteins
	Today's Total:			

Water Log

# of 8-oz. glasses:

1	2	3	4
5	6	7	8
9	10	11	12
13	14	15	16

Mini-Muscle Sets & Activity Log

	# of: Minutes
Activity 1:	
Activity 2:	
Activity 3:	
Activity 4:	
Activity 5:	
Extra Activities:	
Today's Total:	

Energy Log

	Morning	*Afternoon*	*Evening*
High			
Med.			
Low			

TURBOTIP

Once you finish a 10-day period, the value of becoming TurboCharged will be obvious. We know you can do this. Just do it! You belong in the Winner's Circle.

Notes

Today's Date: *Today's Weight:* *Today's Body Fat:* %

WEEK 2 - TUESDAY

Food Log

 # of: Fruits Veggies Proteins

Time: *Food Choice:*

Today's Total:

Mini-Muscle Sets & Activity Log

 # of: Minutes

Activity 1:

Activity 2:

Activity 3:

Activity 4:

Activity 5:

Extra Activities:

Today's Total:

Water Log

# of 8-oz. glasses:

1	2	3	4
5	6	7	8
9	10	11	12
13	14	15	16

Energy Log

	Morning	*Afternoon*	*Evening*
High			
Med.			
Low			

Notes

WEEK 2 - WEDNESDAY

Today's Date: | *Today's Weight:* | *Today's Body Fat:* %

Food Log

 # of: Fruits Veggies Proteins

Time: *Food Choice:*

Today's Total:

Water Log

# of 8-oz. glasses:

1	2	3	4
5	6	7	8
9	10	11	12
13	14	15	16

Mini-Muscle Sets & Activity Log

 # of: Minutes

Activity 1:

Activity 2:

Activity 3:

Activity 4:

Activity 5:

Extra Activities:

Today's Total:

Energy Log

	Morning	*Afternoon*	*Evening*
High			
Med.			
Low			

Notes

Today's Date: *Today's Weight:* *Today's Body Fat:* %

WEEK 2 - THURSDAY

Food Log

of: Fruits Veggies Proteins

Time: *Food Choice:*

Today's Total:

Mini-Muscle Sets & Activity Log

of: Minutes

Activity 1:

Activity 2:

Activity 3:

Activity 4:

Activity 5:

Extra Activities:

Today's Total:

Water Log

# of 8-oz. glasses:

1	2	3	4
5	6	7	8
9	10	11	12
13	14	15	16

Energy Log

	Morning	*Afternoon*	*Evening*
High			
Med.			
Low			

Notes

WEEK 2 - FRIDAY

Today's Date: | *Today's Weight:* | *Today's Body Fat:* %

Food Log

 # of: Fruits Veggies Proteins

Time: *Food Choice:*

Today's Total:

Water Log

# of 8-oz. glasses:

1	2	3	4
5	6	7	8
9	10	11	12
13	14	15	16

Mini-Muscle Sets & Activity Log

 # of: Minutes

Activity 1:

Activity 2:

Activity 3:

Activity 4:

Activity 5:

Extra Activities:

Today's Total:

Energy Log

	Morning	*Afternoon*	*Evening*
High			
Med.			
Low			

Notes

Today's Date: *Today's Weight:* *Today's Body Fat:* %

WEEK 2 - SATURDAY

Food Log

\# of: Fruits Veggies Proteins

Time: *Food Choice:*

Today's Total:

Mini-Muscle Sets & Activity Log

\# of: Minutes

Activity 1:

Activity 2:

Activity 3:

Activity 4:

Activity 5:

Extra Activities:

Today's Total:

Water Log

# of 8-oz. glasses:

1	2	3	4
5	6	7	8
9	10	11	12
13	14	15	16

Energy Log

	Morning	*Afternoon*	*Evening*
High			
Med.			
Low			

Notes

WEEK 2 - SUNDAY

Today's Date: *Today's Weight:*   *Today's Body Fat:* %

Food Log

Time: *Food Choice:*

\# of: Fruits Veggies Proteins

Today's Total:

Water Log

\# of 8-oz. glasses:

1	2	3	4
5	6	7	8
9	10	11	12
13	14	15	16

Mini-Muscle Sets & Activity Log

\# of: Minutes

Activity 1:

Activity 2:

Activity 3:

Activity 4:

Activity 5:

Extra Activities:

Today's Total:

Energy Log

	Morning	*Afternoon*	*Evening*
High			
Med.			
Low			

Notes

WEEK 2 PROGRESS

Activity Wrap-up

Did you meet your activity and mini-muscle strengthening goals for the week?

Starting Weight:

Ending Weight:

Starting Body Fat: %

Ending Body Fat: %

Food Wrap-up

Did you meet your food intake goals for the week?

Energy Wrap-up

Overall, how was your energy level this week?

High ☐

Med. ☐

Low ☐

Goals for Next Week

What things would you like to improve on for next week?

WEEK 3 - MONDAY

Today's Date: | *Today's Weight:* | *Today's Body Fat:* %

Food Log

Time:	*Food Choice:*	# of: Fruits	Veggies	Proteins
	Today's Total:			

Water Log

# of 8-oz. glasses:

1	2	3	4
5	6	7	8
9	10	11	12
13	14	15	16

Energy Log

	Morning	Afternoon	Evening
High			
Med.			
Low			

Mini-Muscle Sets & Activity Log

	# of: Minutes
Activity 1:	
Activity 2:	
Activity 3:	
Activity 4:	
Activity 5:	
Extra Activities:	
Today's Total:	

TURBOTIP

Follow all 8 steps!! Each step is like a part working together with others to create a fully functioning engine.

Notes

Today's Date: *Today's Weight:* *Today's Body Fat:* %

WEEK 3 - TUESDAY

Food Log

Time:	*Food Choice:*	# of: Fruits	Veggies	Proteins
	Today's Total:			

Mini-Muscle Sets & Activity Log

	# of: Minutes
Activity 1:	
Activity 2:	
Activity 3:	
Activity 4:	
Activity 5:	
Extra Activities:	
Today's Total:	

Water Log

# of 8-oz. glasses:

1	2	3	4
5	6	7	8
9	10	11	12
13	14	15	16

Energy Log

	Morning	*Afternoon*	*Evening*
High			
Med.			
Low			

Notes

WEEK 3 - WEDNESDAY

Today's Date: *Today's Weight:* *Today's Body Fat:* %

Food Log

 # of: Fruits Veggies Proteins

Time: *Food Choice:*

Today's Total:

Water Log

# of 8-oz. glasses:

1	2	3	4
5	6	7	8
9	10	11	12
13	14	15	16

Energy Log

	Morning	*Afternoon*	*Evening*
High			
Med.			
Low			

Mini-Muscle Sets & Activity Log

 # of: Minutes

Activity 1:

Activity 2:

Activity 3:

Activity 4:

Activity 5:

Extra Activities:

Today's Total:

Notes

Today's Date: | Today's Weight: | Today's Body Fat: %

WEEK 3 - THURSDAY

Food Log

Time:	Food Choice:	# of: Fruits	Veggies	Proteins
	Today's Total:			

Mini-Muscle Sets & Activity Log

	# of: Minutes
Activity 1:	
Activity 2:	
Activity 3:	
Activity 4:	
Activity 5:	
Extra Activities:	
Today's Total:	

Water Log

of 8-oz. glasses:

1	2	3	4
5	6	7	8
9	10	11	12
13	14	15	16

Energy Log

	Morning	Afternoon	Evening
High			
Med.			
Low			

Notes

WEEK 3 - FRIDAY

Today's Date: ____ *Today's Weight:* ____ *Today's Body Fat:* ____ %

Food Log

Time:	*Food Choice:*	# of: Fruits	Veggies	Proteins
	Today's Total:			

Water Log

# of 8-oz. glasses:

1	2	3	4
5	6	7	8
9	10	11	12
13	14	15	16

Mini-Muscle Sets & Activity Log

	# of: Minutes
Activity 1:	
Activity 2:	
Activity 3:	
Activity 4:	
Activity 5:	
Extra Activities:	
Today's Total:	

Energy Log

	Morning	*Afternoon*	*Evening*
High			
Med.			
Low			

Notes

Today's Date: *Today's Weight:* *Today's Body Fat:* %

WEEK 3 - SATURDAY

Food Log

Time: *Food Choice:*

of: Fruits Veggies Proteins

Today's Total:

Mini-Muscle Sets & Activity Log

of: Minutes

Activity 1:

Activity 2:

Activity 3:

Activity 4:

Activity 5:

Extra Activities:

Today's Total:

Water Log

# of 8-oz. glasses:

1	2	3	4
5	6	7	8
9	10	11	12
13	14	15	16

Energy Log

	Morning	Afternoon	Evening
High			
Med.			
Low			

Notes

WEEK 3 - SUNDAY

Today's Date: | *Today's Weight:* | *Today's Body Fat:* %

Food Log

 # of: Fruits Veggies Proteins

Time: *Food Choice:*

Today's Total:

Water Log

# of 8-oz. glasses:

1	2	3	4
5	6	7	8
9	10	11	12
13	14	15	16

Mini-Muscle Sets & Activity Log

 # of: Minutes

Activity 1:

Activity 2:

Activity 3:

Activity 4:

Activity 5:

Extra Activities:

Today's Total:

Energy Log

	Morning	Afternoon	Evening
High			
Med.			
Low			

Notes

WEEK 3 PROGRESS

Activity Wrap-up

Did you meet your activity and mini-muscle strengthening goals for the week?

Starting Weight:

Ending Weight:

Starting Body Fat: %

Ending Body Fat: %

Food Wrap-up

Did you meet your food intake goals for the week?

Energy Wrap-up

Overall, how was your energy level this week?

High ☐

Med. ☐

Low ☐

Goals for Next Week

What things would you like to improve on for next week?

WEEK 4 - MONDAY

Today's Date: | *Today's Weight:* | *Today's Body Fat:* %

Food Log

Time: *Food Choice:*

of: Fruits Veggies Proteins

Today's Total:

Water Log

# of 8-oz. glasses:

1	2	3	4
5	6	7	8
9	10	11	12
13	14	15	16

Energy Log

	Morning	*Afternoon*	*Evening*
High			
Med.			
Low			

Mini-Muscle Sets & Activity Log

of: Minutes

Activity 1:

Activity 2:

Activity 3:

Activity 4:

Activity 5:

Extra Activities:

Today's Total:

TURBOTIP

What if I make a mistake or blow an entire day? "So what?" we say. Get back in the driver's seat and leave the drama in Hollywood.

Notes

Today's Date: *Today's Weight:*   *Today's Body Fat:* %

WEEK 4 - TUESDAY

Food Log

Time: *Food Choice:*

\# of: Fruits Veggies Proteins

Today's Total:

Mini-Muscle Sets & Activity Log

\# of: Minutes

Activity 1:

Activity 2:

Activity 3:

Activity 4:

Activity 5:

Extra Activities:

Today's Total:

Water Log

# of 8-oz. glasses:

1	2	3	4
5	6	7	8
9	10	11	12
13	14	15	16

Energy Log

	Morning	*Afternoon*	*Evening*
High			
Med.			
Low			

Notes

WEEK 4 - WEDNESDAY

Today's Date: *Today's Weight:* *Today's Body Fat:* %

Food Log

 # of: Fruits Veggies Proteins

Time: *Food Choice:*

Today's Total:

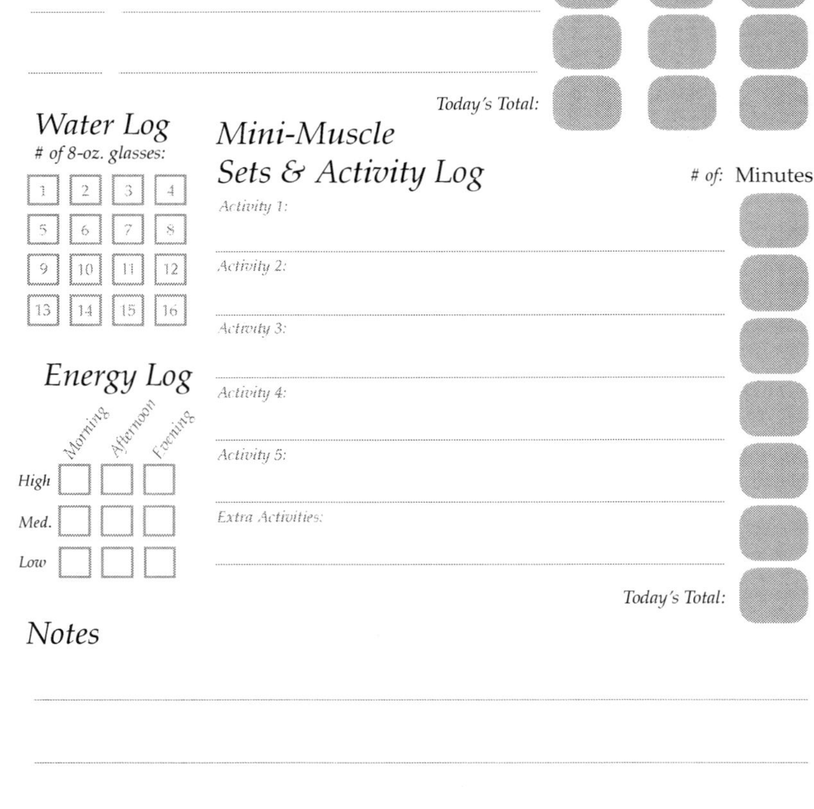

Notes

Today's Date: | Today's Weight: | Today's Body Fat: %

WEEK 4 - THURSDAY

Food Log

Time:	Food Choice:	# of: Fruits	Veggies	Proteins
	Today's Total:			

Mini-Muscle Sets & Activity Log

	# of: Minutes
Activity 1:	
Activity 2:	
Activity 3:	
Activity 4:	
Activity 5:	
Extra Activities:	
Today's Total:	

Water Log

of 8-oz. glasses:

1	2	3	4
5	6	7	8
9	10	11	12
13	14	15	16

Energy Log

	Morning	Afternoon	Evening
High			
Med.			
Low			

Notes

WEEK 4 - FRIDAY

Today's Date: | *Today's Weight:* | *Today's Body Fat:* %

Food Log

Time: *Food Choice:*

# of:	Fruits	Veggies	Proteins
Today's Total:			

Water Log

# of 8-oz. glasses:

1	2	3	4
5	6	7	8
9	10	11	12
13	14	15	16

Energy Log

	Morning	*Afternoon*	*Evening*
High			
Med.			
Low			

Mini-Muscle Sets & Activity Log

 # of: Minutes

Activity 1:

Activity 2:

Activity 3:

Activity 4:

Activity 5:

Extra Activities:

Today's Total:

Notes

Today's Date: Today's Weight: Today's Body Fat: %

WEEK 4 - SATURDAY

Food Log

Time:	Food Choice:	# of: Fruits	Veggies	Proteins
	Today's Total:			

Mini-Muscle Sets & Activity Log

	# of: Minutes
Activity 1:	
Activity 2:	
Activity 3:	
Activity 4:	
Activity 5:	
Extra Activities:	
Today's Total:	

Water Log

of 8-oz. glasses:

1	2	3	4
5	6	7	8
9	10	11	12
13	14	15	16

Energy Log

	Morning	Afternoon	Evening
High			
Med.			
Low			

Notes

WEEK 4 - SUNDAY

Today's Date: *Today's Weight:* *Today's Body Fat:* %

Food Log

 # of: Fruits Veggies Proteins

Time: *Food Choice:*

Today's Total:

Water Log

# of 8-oz. glasses:

1	2	3	4
5	6	7	8
9	10	11	12
13	14	15	16

Mini-Muscle Sets & Activity Log

 # of: Minutes

Activity 1:

Activity 2:

Activity 3:

Activity 4:

Activity 5:

Extra Activities:

Today's Total:

Energy Log

	Morning	*Afternoon*	*Evening*
High			
Med.			
Low			

Notes

WEEK 4 PROGRESS

Activity Wrap-up

Did you meet your activity and mini-muscle strengthening goals for the week?

Starting Weight:

Ending Weight:

Starting Body Fat: %

Ending Body Fat: %

Food Wrap-up

Did you meet your food intake goals for the week?

Energy Wrap-up

Overall, how was your energy level this week?

High ☐

Med. ☐

Low ☐

Goals for Next Week

What things would you like to improve on for next week?

MONTHLY REFLECTION

What changes have you seen in your body, energy, mood, and overall health this month?

MONTHLY PROFILE

Date: ______ *Body Fat:* ______ %

Height: ______ *Neck:* ______ *Waist:* ______ *Hip:* ______ *Weight:* ______

PLACE PHOTO HERE

Notes

WEEK 5 - MONDAY

Today's Date: *Today's Weight:* *Today's Body Fat:* %

Food Log

 # of: Fruits Veggies Proteins

Time: *Food Choice:*

Today's Total:

Water Log

# of 8-oz. glasses:

1	2	3	4
5	6	7	8
9	10	11	12
13	14	15	16

Energy Log

	Morning	Afternoon	Evening
High			
Med.			
Low			

Mini-Muscle Sets & Activity Log

 # of: Minutes

Activity 1:

Activity 2:

Activity 3:

Activity 4:

Activity 5:

Extra Activities:

Today's Total:

Notes

TURBOTIP

If you aren't hungry, don't eat; and when you are hungry, eat enough to feel satisfied!

Today's Date: | Today's Weight: | Today's Body Fat: %

WEEK 5 - TUESDAY

Food Log

Time:	Food Choice:	# of: Fruits	Veggies	Proteins
	Today's Total:			

Mini-Muscle Sets & Activity Log

	# of: Minutes
Activity 1:	
Activity 2:	
Activity 3:	
Activity 4:	
Activity 5:	
Extra Activities:	
Today's Total:	

Water Log

of 8-oz. glasses:

1	2	3	4
5	6	7	8
9	10	11	12
13	14	15	16

Energy Log

	Morning	Afternoon	Evening
High			
Med.			
Low			

Notes

WEEK 5 - WEDNESDAY

Today's Date: | *Today's Weight:* | *Today's Body Fat:* %

Food Log

 # of: Fruits Veggies Proteins

Time: *Food Choice:*

Today's Total:

Water Log

# of 8-oz. glasses:

1	2	3	4
5	6	7	8
9	10	11	12
13	14	15	16

Mini-Muscle Sets & Activity Log

 # of: Minutes

Activity 1:

Activity 2:

Activity 3:

Activity 4:

Activity 5:

Extra Activities:

Today's Total:

Energy Log

	Morning	*Afternoon*	*Evening*
High			
Med.			
Low			

Notes

Today's Date: *Today's Weight:* *Today's Body Fat:* %

WEEK 5 - THURSDAY

Food Log

 # of: Fruits Veggies Proteins

Time: *Food Choice:*

Today's Total:

Mini-Muscle Sets & Activity Log

 # of: Minutes

Activity 1:

Activity 2:

Activity 3:

Activity 4:

Activity 5:

Extra Activities:

Today's Total:

Water Log

# of 8-oz. glasses:

1	2	3	4
5	6	7	8
9	10	11	12
13	14	15	16

Energy Log

	Morning	*Afternoon*	*Evening*
High			
Med.			
Low			

Notes

WEEK 5 - FRIDAY

Today's Date: | *Today's Weight:* | *Today's Body Fat:* %

Food Log

Time:	*Food Choice:*	Fruits	Veggies	Proteins
	Today's Total:			

Water Log

# of 8-oz. glasses:

1	2	3	4
5	6	7	8
9	10	11	12
13	14	15	16

Mini-Muscle Sets & Activity Log

	# of: Minutes
Activity 1:	
Activity 2:	
Activity 3:	
Activity 4:	
Activity 5:	
Extra Activities:	
Today's Total:	

Energy Log

	Morning	*Afternoon*	*Evening*
High			
Med.			
Low			

Notes

Today's Date: *Today's Weight:* *Today's Body Fat:* %

WEEK 5 - SATURDAY

Food Log

\# of: Fruits | Veggies | Proteins

Time: *Food Choice:*

Today's Total:

Mini-Muscle Sets & Activity Log

\# of: Minutes

Activity 1:

Activity 2:

Activity 3:

Activity 4:

Activity 5:

Extra Activities:

Today's Total:

Water Log

# of 8-oz. glasses:

1	2	3	4
5	6	7	8
9	10	11	12
13	14	15	16

Energy Log

	Morning	*Afternoon*	*Evening*
High			
Med.			
Low			

Notes

WEEK 5 - SUNDAY

Today's Date:  *Today's Weight:* *Today's Body Fat:*  %

Food Log

Time:	*Food Choice:*	Fruits	Veggies	Proteins
	Today's Total:			

Water Log

# of 8-oz. glasses:

1	2	3	4
5	6	7	8
9	10	11	12
13	14	15	16

Mini-Muscle Sets & Activity Log

	# of: Minutes
Activity 1:	
Activity 2:	
Activity 3:	
Activity 4:	
Activity 5:	
Extra Activities:	
Today's Total:	

Energy Log

	Morning	*Afternoon*	*Evening*
High			
Med.			
Low			

Notes

WEEK 5 PROGRESS

Activity Wrap-up

Did you meet your activity and mini-muscle strengthening goals for the week?

Starting Weight:

Ending Weight:

Starting Body Fat: %

Ending Body Fat: %

Food Wrap-up

Did you meet your food intake goals for the week?

Energy Wrap-up

Overall, how was your energy level this week?

High ☐

Med. ☐

Low ☐

Goals for Next Week

What things would you like to improve on for next week?

WEEK 6 - MONDAY

Today's Date: *Today's Weight:*   *Today's Body Fat:* %

Food Log

Time:	*Food Choice:*	Fruits	Veggies	Proteins
	Today's Total:			

Water Log

# of 8-oz. glasses:

1	2	3	4
5	6	7	8
9	10	11	12
13	14	15	16

Energy Log

	Morning	Afternoon	Evening
High			
Med.			
Low			

Mini-Muscle Sets & Activity Log

	# of: Minutes
Activity 1:	
Activity 2:	
Activity 3:	
Activity 4:	
Activity 5:	
Extra Activities:	
Today's Total:	

TURBOTIP

You need to do 3-5 Mini-Muscle Sessions everyday to maintain your lean body mass. You want to lose your fat, while maintaining your muscles.

Notes

Today's Date: *Today's Weight:* *Today's Body Fat:* %

WEEK 6 - TUESDAY

Food Log

 # of: Fruits Veggies Proteins

Time: *Food Choice:*

Today's Total:

Mini-Muscle Sets & Activity Log

 # of: Minutes

Activity 1:

Activity 2:

Activity 3:

Activity 4:

Activity 5:

Extra Activities:

Today's Total:

Water Log

# of 8-oz. glasses:

1	2	3	4
5	6	7	8
9	10	11	12
13	14	15	16

Energy Log

	Morning	*Afternoon*	*Evening*
High			
Med.			
Low			

Notes

WEEK 6 - WEDNESDAY

Today's Date: *Today's Weight:* *Today's Body Fat:* %

Food Log

Time: *Food Choice:*

# of:	Fruits	Veggies	Proteins
Today's Total:			

Water Log

# of 8-oz. glasses:

1	2	3	4
5	6	7	8
9	10	11	12
13	14	15	16

Energy Log

	Morning	*Afternoon*	*Evening*
High			
Med.			
Low			

Mini-Muscle Sets & Activity Log

	# of: Minutes
Activity 1:	
Activity 2:	
Activity 3:	
Activity 4:	
Activity 5:	
Extra Activities:	
Today's Total:	

Notes

Today's Date: | Today's Weight: | Today's Body Fat: %

WEEK 6 - THURSDAY

Food Log

of: Fruits | Veggies | Proteins

Time: | Food Choice:

Today's Total:

Mini-Muscle Sets & Activity Log

of: Minutes

Activity 1:

Activity 2:

Activity 3:

Activity 4:

Activity 5:

Extra Activities:

Today's Total:

Water Log

of 8-oz. glasses:

1	2	3	4
5	6	7	8
9	10	11	12
13	14	15	16

Energy Log

	Morning	Afternoon	Evening
High			
Med.			
Low			

Notes

WEEK 6 - FRIDAY

Today's Date:

Today's Weight:

Today's Body Fat: %

Food Log

Time:	*Food Choice:*	# of: Fruits	Veggies	Proteins
	Today's Total:			

Water Log

# of 8-oz. glasses:

1	2	3	4
5	6	7	8
9	10	11	12
13	14	15	16

Mini-Muscle Sets & Activity Log

	# of: Minutes
Activity 1:	
Activity 2:	
Activity 3:	
Activity 4:	
Activity 5:	
Extra Activities:	
Today's Total:	

Energy Log

	Morning	*Afternoon*	*Evening*
High			
Med.			
Low			

Notes

Today's Date: *Today's Weight:*   *Today's Body Fat:* %

WEEK 6 - SATURDAY

Food Log

Time: *Food Choice:*

\# of: Fruits Veggies Proteins

Today's Total:

Mini-Muscle Sets & Activity Log

\# of: Minutes

Activity 1:

Activity 2:

Activity 3:

Activity 4:

Activity 5:

Extra Activities:

Today's Total:

Water Log

# of 8-oz. glasses:

1	2	3	4
5	6	7	8
9	10	11	12
13	14	15	16

Energy Log

	Morning	*Afternoon*	*Evening*
High			
Med.			
Low			

Notes

WEEK 6 - SUNDAY

Today's Date:  Today's Weight: Today's Body Fat:  %

Food Log

Time:	Food Choice:	# of: Fruits	Veggies	Proteins
	Today's Total:			

Water Log

of 8-oz. glasses:

1	2	3	4
5	6	7	8
9	10	11	12
13	14	15	16

Mini-Muscle Sets & Activity Log

	# of: Minutes
Activity 1:	
Activity 2:	
Activity 3:	
Activity 4:	
Activity 5:	
Extra Activities:	
Today's Total:	

Energy Log

	Morning	Afternoon	Evening
High			
Med.			
Low			

Notes

WEEK 6 PROGRESS

Activity Wrap-up

Did you meet your activity and mini-muscle strengthening goals for the week?

Starting Weight:

Ending Weight:

Starting Body Fat: %

Ending Body Fat: %

Food Wrap-up

Did you meet your food intake goals for the week?

Energy Wrap-up

Overall, how was your energy level this week?

High ☐

Med. ☐

Low ☐

Goals for Next Week

What things would you like to improve on for next week?

WEEK 7 - MONDAY

Today's Date: | *Today's Weight:* | *Today's Body Fat:* %

Food Log

Time: *Food Choice:*

 # of: Fruits Veggies Proteins

Today's Total:

Water Log

# of 8-oz. glasses:

1	2	3	4
5	6	7	8
9	10	11	12
13	14	15	16

Mini-Muscle Sets & Activity Log

 # of: Minutes

Activity 1:

Activity 2:

Activity 3:

Activity 4:

Activity 5:

Extra Activities:

Today's Total:

Energy Log

	Morning	*Afternoon*	*Evening*
High			
Med.			
Low			

Notes

TURBOTIP

Food that is nutritionally potent will satisfy you and will make you feel really, really good.

Today's Date: *Today's Weight:* *Today's Body Fat:* %

WEEK 7 - TUESDAY

Food Log

Time: *Food Choice:*

\# *of:* Fruits Veggies Proteins

Today's Total:

Mini-Muscle Sets & Activity Log

\# *of:* Minutes

Activity 1:

Activity 2:

Activity 3:

Activity 4:

Activity 5:

Extra Activities:

Today's Total:

Water Log

\# *of 8-oz. glasses:*

1	2	3	4
5	6	7	8
9	10	11	12
13	14	15	16

Energy Log

	Morning	*Afternoon*	*Evening*
High			
Med.			
Low			

Notes

WEEK 7 - WEDNESDAY

Today's Date: | *Today's Weight:* | *Today's Body Fat:* %

Food Log

Time:	*Food Choice:*	Fruits	Veggies	Proteins
	Today's Total:			

Water Log

# of 8-oz. glasses:

1	2	3	4
5	6	7	8
9	10	11	12
13	14	15	16

Energy Log

	Morning	Afternoon	Evening
High			
Med.			
Low			

Mini-Muscle Sets & Activity Log

	# of: Minutes
Activity 1:	
Activity 2:	
Activity 3:	
Activity 4:	
Activity 5:	
Extra Activities:	
Today's Total:	

Notes

Today's Date: ______ *Today's Weight:* ______ *Today's Body Fat:* ______ %

WEEK 7 - THURSDAY

Food Log

Time:	*Food Choice:*	# of: Fruits	Veggies	Proteins
	Today's Total:			

Mini-Muscle Sets & Activity Log

	# of: Minutes
Activity 1:	
Activity 2:	
Activity 3:	
Activity 4:	
Activity 5:	
Extra Activities:	
Today's Total:	

Water Log

# of 8-oz. glasses:

1	2	3	4
5	6	7	8
9	10	11	12
13	14	15	16

Energy Log

	Morning	*Afternoon*	*Evening*
High			
Med.			
Low			

Notes

WEEK 7 - FRIDAY

Today's Date: *Today's Weight:*   *Today's Body Fat:* %

Food Log

Time:	*Food Choice:*	*# of:* Fruits	Veggies	Proteins
	Today's Total:			

Water Log

# of 8-oz. glasses:

1	2	3	4
5	6	7	8
9	10	11	12
13	14	15	16

Energy Log

	Morning	*Afternoon*	*Evening*
High			
Med.			
Low			

Mini-Muscle Sets & Activity Log

	# of: Minutes
Activity 1:	
Activity 2:	
Activity 3:	
Activity 4:	
Activity 5:	
Extra Activities:	
Today's Total:	

Notes

Today's Date: *Today's Weight:* *Today's Body Fat:* %

WEEK 7 - SATURDAY

Food Log

Time: *Food Choice:*

\# of: Fruits Veggies Proteins

Today's Total:

Mini-Muscle Sets & Activity Log

\# of: Minutes

Activity 1:

Activity 2:

Activity 3:

Activity 4:

Activity 5:

Extra Activities:

Today's Total:

Water Log

# of 8-oz. glasses:

1	2	3	4
5	6	7	8
9	10	11	12
13	14	15	16

Energy Log

	Morning	*Afternoon*	*Evening*
High			
Med.			
Low			

Notes

WEEK 7 - SUNDAY

Today's Date: | *Today's Weight:* | *Today's Body Fat:* %

Food Log

 # of: Fruits | Veggies | Proteins

Time: *Food Choice:*

Today's Total:

Water Log

# of 8-oz. glasses:

1	2	3	4
5	6	7	8
9	10	11	12
13	14	15	16

Energy Log

	Morning	*Afternoon*	*Evening*
High			
Med.			
Low			

Mini-Muscle Sets & Activity Log

 # of: Minutes

Activity 1:

Activity 2:

Activity 3:

Activity 4:

Activity 5:

Extra Activities:

Today's Total:

Notes

WEEK 7 PROGRESS

Activity Wrap-up

Did you meet your activity and mini-muscle strengthening goals for the week?

Starting Weight:

Ending Weight:

Starting Body Fat: %

Ending Body Fat: %

Food Wrap-up

Did you meet your food intake goals for the week?

Energy Wrap-up

Overall, how was your energy level this week?

- *High* ☐
- *Med.* ☐
- *Low* ☐

Goals for Next Week

What things would you like to improve on for next week?

WEEK 8 - MONDAY

Today's Date: | *Today's Weight:* | *Today's Body Fat:* %

Food Log

Time: *Food Choice:*

 # of: Fruits Veggies Proteins

Today's Total:

Water Log

# of 8-oz. glasses:

1	2	3	4
5	6	7	8
9	10	11	12
13	14	15	16

Energy Log

	Morning	*Afternoon*	*Evening*
High			
Med.			
Low			

Mini-Muscle Sets & Activity Log

 # of: Minutes

Activity 1:

Activity 2:

Activity 3:

Activity 4:

Activity 5:

Extra Activities:

Today's Total:

TURBOTIP

A moderate and consistent increase in your daily activity, day after day, is much more effective than random spurts on the weekend.

Notes

Today's Date: *Today's Weight:* *Today's Body Fat:* %

WEEK 8 - TUESDAY

Food Log

\# of: Fruits Veggies Proteins

Time: *Food Choice:*

Today's Total:

Mini-Muscle Sets & Activity Log

\# of: Minutes

Activity 1:

Activity 2:

Activity 3:

Activity 4:

Activity 5:

Extra Activities:

Today's Total:

Water Log

# of 8-oz. glasses:

1	2	3	4
5	6	7	8
9	10	11	12
13	14	15	16

Energy Log

	Morning	*Afternoon*	*Evening*
High			
Med.			
Low			

Notes

WEEK 8 - WEDNESDAY

Today's Date: *Today's Weight:* *Today's Body Fat:* %

Food Log

Time: *Food Choice:*

\# of: Fruits Veggies Proteins

Today's Total:

Water Log

# of 8-oz. glasses:

1	2	3	4
5	6	7	8
9	10	11	12
13	14	15	16

Energy Log

	Morning	Afternoon	Evening
High			
Med.			
Low			

Mini-Muscle Sets & Activity Log

\# of: Minutes

Activity 1:

Activity 2:

Activity 3:

Activity 4:

Activity 5:

Extra Activities:

Today's Total:

Notes

Today's Date: | *Today's Weight:* | *Today's Body Fat:* %

WEEK 8 - THURSDAY

Food Log

Time: | *Food Choice:* | # of: Fruits | Veggies | Proteins

Today's Total:

Mini-Muscle Sets & Activity Log

of: Minutes

Activity 1:

Activity 2:

Activity 3:

Activity 4:

Activity 5:

Extra Activities:

Today's Total:

Water Log

# of 8-oz. glasses:

1	2	3	4
5	6	7	8
9	10	11	12
13	14	15	16

Energy Log

	Morning	*Afternoon*	*Evening*
High			
Med.			
Low			

Notes

WEEK 8 - FRIDAY

Food Log

Time:	Food Choice:	# of: Fruits	Veggies	Proteins
	Today's Total:			

Water Log

\# of 8-oz. glasses:

1	2	3	4
5	6	7	8
9	10	11	12
13	14	15	16

Energy Log

	Morning	Afternoon	Evening
High			
Med.			
Low			

Mini-Muscle Sets & Activity Log

	# of: Minutes
Activity 1:	
Activity 2:	
Activity 3:	
Activity 4:	
Activity 5:	
Extra Activities:	
Today's Total:	

Notes

Today's Date: *Today's Weight:* *Today's Body Fat:* %

WEEK 8 - SATURDAY

Food Log

Time: *Food Choice:*

of: Fruits Veggies Proteins

Today's Total:

Mini-Muscle Sets & Activity Log

of: Minutes

Activity 1:

Activity 2:

Activity 3:

Activity 4:

Activity 5:

Extra Activities:

Today's Total:

Water Log

# of 8-oz. glasses:

1	2	3	4
5	6	7	8
9	10	11	12
13	14	15	16

Energy Log

	Morning	*Afternoon*	*Evening*
High			
Med.			
Low			

Notes

WEEK 8 - SUNDAY

Today's Date: | *Today's Weight:* | *Today's Body Fat:* %

Food Log

 # of: Fruits Veggies Proteins

Time: *Food Choice:*

Today's Total:

Water Log

# of 8-oz. glasses:

1	2	3	4
5	6	7	8
9	10	11	12
13	14	15	16

Energy Log

	Morning	*Afternoon*	*Evening*
High			
Med.			
Low			

Mini-Muscle Sets & Activity Log

 # of: Minutes

Activity 1:

Activity 2:

Activity 3:

Activity 4:

Activity 5:

Extra Activities:

Today's Total:

Notes

WEEK 8 PROGRESS

Activity Wrap-up

Did you meet your activity and mini-muscle strengthening goals for the week?

Starting Weight:

Ending Weight:

Starting Body Fat: %

Ending Body Fat: %

Food Wrap-up

Did you meet your food intake goals for the week?

Energy Wrap-up

Overall, how was your energy level this week?

High ☐

Med. ☐

Low ☐

Goals for Next Week

What things would you like to improve on for next week?

MONTHLY REFLECTION

What changes have you seen in your body, energy, mood, and overall health this month?

Date: Body Fat: %

MONTHLY PROFILE

Height: Neck: Waist: Hip: Weight:

PLACE PHOTO HERE

Notes

WEEK 9 - MONDAY

Today's Date: *Today's Weight:* *Today's Body Fat:* %

Food Log

Time:	*Food Choice:*	Fruits	Veggies	Proteins
	Today's Total:			

Water Log

# of 8-oz. glasses:

1	2	3	4
5	6	7	8
9	10	11	12
13	14	15	16

Energy Log

	Morning	Afternoon	Evening
High			
Med.			
Low			

Mini-Muscle Sets & Activity Log

	# of: Minutes
Activity 1:	
Activity 2:	
Activity 3:	
Activity 4:	
Activity 5:	
Extra Activities:	
Today's Total:	

Notes

TURBOTIP

Walking favorably alters cholesterol, blood sugar, insulin, triglycerides, and blood pressure.

Today's Date: *Today's Weight:* *Today's Body Fat:* %

WEEK 9 - TUESDAY

Food Log

 # of: Fruits Veggies Proteins

Time: *Food Choice:*

Today's Total:

Mini-Muscle Sets & Activity Log

 # of: Minutes

Activity 1:

Activity 2:

Activity 3:

Activity 4:

Activity 5:

Extra Activities:

Today's Total:

Water Log

# of 8-oz. glasses:

1	2	3	4
5	6	7	8
9	10	11	12
13	14	15	16

Energy Log

	Morning	*Afternoon*	*Evening*
High			
Med.			
Low			

Notes

WEEK 9 - WEDNESDAY

Today's Date: *Today's Weight:* *Today's Body Fat:* %

Food Log

 # of: Fruits Veggies Proteins

Time: *Food Choice:*

Today's Total:

Water Log

# of 8-oz. glasses:

1	2	3	4
5	6	7	8
9	10	11	12
13	14	15	16

Mini-Muscle Sets & Activity Log

 # of: Minutes

Activity 1:

Activity 2:

Activity 3:

Activity 4:

Activity 5:

Extra Activities:

Today's Total:

Energy Log

	Morning	Afternoon	Evening
High			
Med.			
Low			

Notes

Today's Date: | Today's Weight: | Today's Body Fat: %

WEEK 9 - THURSDAY

Food Log

Time: | Food Choice: | # of: Fruits | Veggies | Proteins

Today's Total:

Mini-Muscle Sets & Activity Log

of: Minutes

Activity 1:

Activity 2:

Activity 3:

Activity 4:

Activity 5:

Extra Activities:

Today's Total:

Water Log

of 8-oz. glasses:

1	2	3	4
5	6	7	8
9	10	11	12
13	14	15	16

Energy Log

	Morning	Afternoon	Evening
High			
Med.			
Low			

Notes

WEEK 9 - FRIDAY

Today's Date: *Today's Weight:* *Today's Body Fat:* %

Food Log

 # of: Fruits Veggies Proteins

Time: *Food Choice:*

Today's Total:

Water Log

# of 8-oz. glasses:

1	2	3	4
5	6	7	8
9	10	11	12
13	14	15	16

Energy Log

	Morning	*Afternoon*	*Evening*
High			
Med.			
Low			

Mini-Muscle Sets & Activity Log

 # of: Minutes

Activity 1:

Activity 2:

Activity 3:

Activity 4:

Activity 5:

Extra Activities:

Today's Total:

Notes

Today's Date: *Today's Weight:* *Today's Body Fat:* %

WEEK 9 - SATURDAY

Food Log

\# of: Fruits Veggies Proteins

Time: *Food Choice:*

Today's Total:

Mini-Muscle Sets & Activity Log

\# of: Minutes

Activity 1:

Activity 2:

Activity 3:

Activity 4:

Activity 5:

Extra Activities:

Today's Total:

Water Log

# of 8-oz. glasses:

1	2	3	4
5	6	7	8
9	10	11	12
13	14	15	16

Energy Log

	Morning	*Afternoon*	*Evening*
High			
Med.			
Low			

Notes

WEEK 9 - SUNDAY

Today's Date: | *Today's Weight:* | *Today's Body Fat:* %

Food Log

 # of: Fruits Veggies Proteins

Time:	*Food Choice:*	Fruits	Veggies	Proteins
	Today's Total:			

Water Log

# of 8-oz. glasses:

1	2	3	4
5	6	7	8
9	10	11	12
13	14	15	16

Energy Log

	Morning	*Afternoon*	*Evening*
High			
Med.			
Low			

Mini-Muscle Sets & Activity Log

	# of: Minutes
Activity 1:	
Activity 2:	
Activity 3:	
Activity 4:	
Activity 5:	
Extra Activities:	
Today's Total:	

Notes

WEEK 9 PROGRESS

Activity Wrap-up

Did you meet your activity and mini-muscle strengthening goals for the week?

Starting Weight:

Ending Weight:

Starting Body Fat: %

Ending Body Fat: %

Food Wrap-up

Did you meet your food intake goals for the week?

Energy Wrap-up

Overall, how was your energy level this week?

High ☐

Med. ☐

Low ☐

Goals for Next Week

What things would you like to improve on for next week?

WEEK 10 - MONDAY

Today's Date: *Today's Weight:* *Today's Body Fat:* %

Food Log

Time: *Food Choice:*

of: Fruits Veggies Proteins

Today's Total:

Water Log

# of 8-oz. glasses:

1	2	3	4
5	6	7	8
9	10	11	12
13	14	15	16

Mini-Muscle Sets & Activity Log

 # of: Minutes

Activity 1:

Activity 2:

Activity 3:

Activity 4:

Activity 5:

Extra Activities:

Today's Total:

Energy Log

	Morning	*Afternoon*	*Evening*
High			
Med.			
Low			

TURBOTIP

The 8 simple TurboCharged steps will stand the test of time because they work with your body and not against it.

Notes

Today's Date: *Today's Weight:* *Today's Body Fat:* %

WEEK 10 - TUESDAY

Food Log

Time: *Food Choice:*

of: Fruits Veggies Proteins

Today's Total:

Mini-Muscle Sets & Activity Log

Activity 1:

Activity 2:

Activity 3:

Activity 4:

Activity 5:

Extra Activities:

of: Minutes

Today's Total:

Water Log

# of 8-oz. glasses:

1	2	3	4
5	6	7	8
9	10	11	12
13	14	15	16

Energy Log

	Morning	*Afternoon*	*Evening*
High			
Med.			
Low			

Notes

WEEK 10 - WEDNESDAY

Today's Date: | *Today's Weight:* | *Today's Body Fat:* %

Food Log

Time: *Food Choice:*

# of:	Fruits	Veggies	Proteins
Today's Total:			

Water Log

# of 8-oz. glasses:

1	2	3	4
5	6	7	8
9	10	11	12
13	14	15	16

Mini-Muscle Sets & Activity Log

	# of: Minutes
Activity 1:	
Activity 2:	
Activity 3:	
Activity 4:	
Activity 5:	
Extra Activities:	
Today's Total:	

Energy Log

	Morning	*Afternoon*	*Evening*
High			
Med.			
Low			

Notes

Today's Date: | *Today's Weight:* | *Today's Body Fat:* %

WEEK 10 - THURSDAY

Food Log

Time: | *Food Choice:*

of: Fruits | Veggies | Proteins

Today's Total:

Mini-Muscle Sets & Activity Log

of: Minutes

Activity 1:

Activity 2:

Activity 3:

Activity 4:

Activity 5:

Extra Activities:

Today's Total:

Water Log

# of 8-oz. glasses:

1	2	3	4
5	6	7	8
9	10	11	12
13	14	15	16

Energy Log

	Morning	*Afternoon*	*Evening*
High			
Med.			
Low			

Notes

WEEK 10 - FRIDAY

Today's Date: *Today's Weight:*   *Today's Body Fat:* %

Food Log

Time:	*Food Choice:*	*# of:* Fruits	Veggies	Proteins
	Today's Total:			

Water Log

# of 8-oz. glasses:

1	2	3	4
5	6	7	8
9	10	11	12
13	14	15	16

Energy Log

	Morning	*Afternoon*	*Evening*
High			
Med.			
Low			

Mini-Muscle Sets & Activity Log

	# of: Minutes
Activity 1:	
Activity 2:	
Activity 3:	
Activity 4:	
Activity 5:	
Extra Activities:	
Today's Total:	

Notes

Today's Date: | Today's Weight: | Today's Body Fat: %

WEEK 10 - SATURDAY

Food Log

Time: | Food Choice: | # of: Fruits | Veggies | Proteins

Today's Total:

Mini-Muscle Sets & Activity Log

of: Minutes

Activity 1:

Activity 2:

Activity 3:

Activity 4:

Activity 5:

Extra Activities:

Today's Total:

Water Log

\# of 8-oz. glasses:

1	2	3	4
5	6	7	8
9	10	11	12
13	14	15	16

Energy Log

	Morning	Afternoon	Evening
High			
Med.			
Low			

Notes

WEEK 10 - SUNDAY

Today's Date: *Today's Weight:*   *Today's Body Fat:* %

Food Log

Time: *Food Choice:*

 # of: Fruits Veggies Proteins

Today's Total:

Water Log

# of 8-oz. glasses:

1	2	3	4
5	6	7	8
9	10	11	12
13	14	15	16

Mini-Muscle Sets & Activity Log

 # of: Minutes

Activity 1:

Activity 2:

Activity 3:

Activity 4:

Activity 5:

Extra Activities:

Today's Total:

Energy Log

	Morning	*Afternoon*	*Evening*
High			
Med.			
Low			

Notes

WEEK 10 PROGRESS

Activity Wrap-up

Did you meet your activity and mini-muscle strengthening goals for the week?

Starting Weight:

Ending Weight:

Starting Body Fat: %

Ending Body Fat: %

Food Wrap-up

Did you meet your food intake goals for the week?

Energy Wrap-up

Overall, how was your energy level this week?

High ☐

Med. ☐

Low ☐

Goals for Next Week

What things would you like to improve on for next week?

WEEK 11 - MONDAY

Today's Date: *Today's Weight:* *Today's Body Fat:* %

Food Log

 # of: Fruits Veggies Proteins

Time: *Food Choice:*

Today's Total:

Water Log

# of 8-oz. glasses:

1	2	3	4
5	6	7	8
9	10	11	12
13	14	15	16

Energy Log

	Morning	*Afternoon*	*Evening*
High			
Med.			
Low			

Mini-Muscle Sets & Activity Log

 # of: Minutes

Activity 1:

Activity 2:

Activity 3:

Activity 4:

Activity 5:

Extra Activities:

Today's Total:

Notes

TURBOTIP

Imagining your new sleek body will help you avoid temptations and potential crashes.

Today's Date: | Today's Weight: | Today's Body Fat: %

WEEK 11 - TUESDAY

Food Log

Time: *Food Choice:*

# of:	Fruits	Veggies	Proteins
Today's Total:			

Mini-Muscle Sets & Activity Log

	# of: Minutes
Activity 1:	
Activity 2:	
Activity 3:	
Activity 4:	
Activity 5:	
Extra Activities:	
Today's Total:	

Water Log

# of 8-oz. glasses:

1	2	3	4
5	6	7	8
9	10	11	12
13	14	15	16

Energy Log

	Morning	*Afternoon*	*Evening*
High			
Med.			
Low			

Notes

WEEK 11 - WEDNESDAY

Today's Date: *Today's Weight:* *Today's Body Fat:* %

Food Log

Time: *Food Choice:*

\# of: Fruits Veggies Proteins

Today's Total:

Water Log

# of 8-oz. glasses:

1	2	3	4
5	6	7	8
9	10	11	12
13	14	15	16

Energy Log

	Morning	Afternoon	Evening
High			
Med.			
Low			

Mini-Muscle Sets & Activity Log

\# of: Minutes

Activity 1:

Activity 2:

Activity 3:

Activity 4:

Activity 5:

Extra Activities:

Today's Total:

Notes

Today's Date: | Today's Weight: | Today's Body Fat: %

WEEK 11 - THURSDAY

Food Log

Time:	Food Choice:	# of: Fruits	Veggies	Proteins
	Today's Total:			

Mini-Muscle Sets & Activity Log

	# of: Minutes
Activity 1:	
Activity 2:	
Activity 3:	
Activity 4:	
Activity 5:	
Extra Activities:	
Today's Total:	

Water Log

\# of 8-oz. glasses:

1	2	3	4
5	6	7	8
9	10	11	12
13	14	15	16

Energy Log

	Morning	Afternoon	Evening
High			
Med.			
Low			

Notes

WEEK 11 - FRIDAY

Today's Date: | *Today's Weight:* | *Today's Body Fat:* %

Food Log

Time:	*Food Choice:*	# of: Fruits	Veggies	Proteins
	Today's Total:			

Water Log

# of 8-oz. glasses:

1	2	3	4
5	6	7	8
9	10	11	12
13	14	15	16

Energy Log

	Morning	Afternoon	Evening
High			
Med.			
Low			

Mini-Muscle Sets & Activity Log

	# of: Minutes
Activity 1:	
Activity 2:	
Activity 3:	
Activity 4:	
Activity 5:	
Extra Activities:	
Today's Total:	

Notes

Today's Date: | *Today's Weight:* | *Today's Body Fat:* %

WEEK 11 - SATURDAY

Food Log

Time:	*Food Choice:*	# of: Fruits	Veggies	Proteins
	Today's Total:			

Mini-Muscle Sets & Activity Log

	# of: Minutes
Activity 1:	
Activity 2:	
Activity 3:	
Activity 4:	
Activity 5:	
Extra Activities:	
Today's Total:	

Water Log

# of 8-oz. glasses:

1	2	3	4
5	6	7	8
9	10	11	12
13	14	15	16

Energy Log

	Morning	*Afternoon*	*Evening*
High			
Med.			
Low			

Notes

WEEK 11 - SUNDAY

Today's Date: | *Today's Weight:* | *Today's Body Fat:* %

Food Log

Time: *Food Choice:*

 # of: Fruits Veggies Proteins

Today's Total:

Water Log

# of 8-oz. glasses:

1	2	3	4
5	6	7	8
9	10	11	12
13	14	15	16

Mini-Muscle Sets & Activity Log

 # of: Minutes

Activity 1:

Activity 2:

Activity 3:

Activity 4:

Activity 5:

Extra Activities:

Today's Total:

Energy Log

	Morning	*Afternoon*	*Evening*
High			
Med.			
Low			

Notes

WEEK 11 PROGRESS

Activity Wrap-up

Did you meet your activity and mini-muscle strengthening goals for the week?

Starting Weight:

Ending Weight:

Starting Body Fat: %

Ending Body Fat: %

Food Wrap-up

Did you meet your food intake goals for the week?

Energy Wrap-up

Overall, how was your energy level this week?

High ☐

Med. ☐

Low ☐

Goals for Next Week

What things would you like to improve on for next week?

WEEK 12 - MONDAY

Today's Date: *Today's Weight:* *Today's Body Fat:* %

Food Log

Time: *Food Choice:*

\# of: Fruits Veggies Proteins

Today's Total:

Water Log

# of 8-oz. glasses:

1	2	3	4
5	6	7	8
9	10	11	12
13	14	15	16

Mini-Muscle Sets & Activity Log

\# of: Minutes

Activity 1:

Activity 2:

Activity 3:

Activity 4:

Activity 5:

Extra Activities:

Today's Total:

Energy Log

	Morning	*Afternoon*	*Evening*
High			
Med.			
Low			

Notes

TURBOTIP

Success in any endeavor is not about perfection. Success is all about consistency.

Today's Date: Today's Weight: Today's Body Fat: %

WEEK 12 - TUESDAY

Food Log

Time:	Food Choice:	# of: Fruits	Veggies	Proteins
	Today's Total:			

Mini-Muscle Sets & Activity Log

	# of: Minutes
Activity 1:	
Activity 2:	
Activity 3:	
Activity 4:	
Activity 5:	
Extra Activities:	
Today's Total:	

Water Log

of 8-oz. glasses:

1	2	3	4
5	6	7	8
9	10	11	12
13	14	15	16

Energy Log

	Morning	Afternoon	Evening
High			
Med.			
Low			

Notes

WEEK 12 - WEDNESDAY

Today's Date: | *Today's Weight:* | *Today's Body Fat:* %

Food Log

Time:	*Food Choice:*	# of: Fruits	Veggies	Proteins
	Today's Total:			

Water Log

# of 8-oz. glasses:

1	2	3	4
5	6	7	8
9	10	11	12
13	14	15	16

Energy Log

	Morning	*Afternoon*	*Evening*
High			
Med.			
Low			

Mini-Muscle Sets & Activity Log

	# of: Minutes
Activity 1:	
Activity 2:	
Activity 3:	
Activity 4:	
Activity 5:	
Extra Activities:	
Today's Total:	

Notes

Today's Date: *Today's Weight:* *Today's Body Fat:* %

WEEK 12 - THURSDAY

Food Log

Time: *Food Choice:*

of: Fruits Veggies Proteins

Today's Total:

Mini-Muscle Sets & Activity Log

of: Minutes

Activity 1:

Activity 2:

Activity 3:

Activity 4:

Activity 5:

Extra Activities:

Today's Total:

Water Log

# of 8-oz. glasses:

1	2	3	4
5	6	7	8
9	10	11	12
13	14	15	16

Energy Log

	Morning	*Afternoon*	*Evening*
High			
Med.			
Low			

Notes

WEEK 12 - FRIDAY

Today's Date: *Today's Weight:* *Today's Body Fat:* %

Food Log

\# of: Fruits Veggies Proteins

Time: *Food Choice:*

Today's Total:

Water Log

# of 8-oz. glasses:

1	2	3	4
5	6	7	8
9	10	11	12
13	14	15	16

Mini-Muscle Sets & Activity Log

\# of: Minutes

Activity 1:

Activity 2:

Activity 3:

Activity 4:

Activity 5:

Extra Activities:

Today's Total:

Energy Log

	Morning	*Afternoon*	*Evening*
High			
Med.			
Low			

Notes

Today's Date: | Today's Weight: | Today's Body Fat: %

WEEK 12 - SATURDAY

Food Log

Time:	Food Choice:	# of: Fruits	Veggies	Proteins
	Today's Total:			

Mini-Muscle Sets & Activity Log

	# of: Minutes
Activity 1:	
Activity 2:	
Activity 3:	
Activity 4:	
Activity 5:	
Extra Activities:	
Today's Total:	

Water Log

of 8-oz. glasses:

1	2	3	4
5	6	7	8
9	10	11	12
13	14	15	16

Energy Log

	Morning	Afternoon	Evening
High			
Med.			
Low			

Notes

WEEK 12 - SUNDAY

Today's Date: *Today's Weight:*   *Today's Body Fat:* %

Food Log

 # of: Fruits Veggies Proteins

Time:	*Food Choice:*	Fruits	Veggies	Proteins
	Today's Total:			

Water Log

# of 8-oz. glasses:

1	2	3	4
5	6	7	8
9	10	11	12
13	14	15	16

Mini-Muscle Sets & Activity Log

 # of: Minutes

Activity 1:

Activity 2:

Activity 3:

Activity 4:

Activity 5:

Extra Activities:

Today's Total:

Energy Log

	Morning	*Afternoon*	*Evening*
High			
Med.			
Low			

Notes

WEEK 12 PROGRESS

Activity Wrap-up

Did you meet your activity and mini-muscle strengthening goals for the week?

Starting Weight:

Ending Weight:

Starting Body Fat: %

Ending Body Fat: %

Food Wrap-up

Did you meet your food intake goals for the week?

Energy Wrap-up

Overall, how was your energy level this week?

High ☐

Med. ☐

Low ☐

Goals for Next Week

What things would you like to improve on for next week?

Month 1 Starting Measurements:

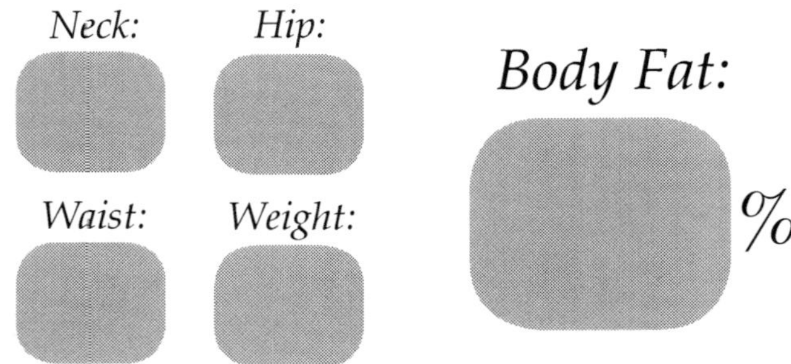

Month 3 Ending Measurements:

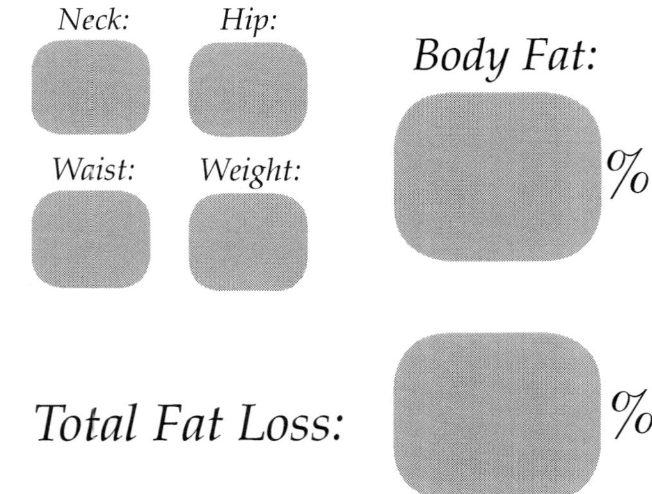

Total Fat Loss: %

Results

....

....

....

....

PLACE PHOTO HERE

Notes

P.S. Congrats on getting TurboCharged! -Dian & Tom